HOW TO SELF-PUBLISH
YOUR BOOK
2nd Edition

Also by Mateja Klaric

Self-Publishing Made Easy

You Self-Published, Now What?
How to Promote Your Book

How to Create Your Website:
For Writers and Other Clueless Souls

The Fox & White Rabbit

The Story of the Fox and White Rabbit
(not your ordinary fable)

HOW TO SELF-PUBLISH YOUR BOOK

The Fast, Free & Easy Way

2nd Edition

Mateja Klaric

How to Self-Publish Your Book: The Fast, Free & Easy Way
Second edition, November 29, 2018, published by Mateja Klaric
First book in the series *Self-Publishing Made Easy*
ISBN: 9781790459759

Author: Mateja Klaric
Proofreading: James Reeves
Cover & book design: Mateja Klaric

Dedicated to all those who have stood by my side
in the time of need. Thank you for your
invaluable help and support.

Special thanks to James Reeves, my patron on Patreon.

TABLE OF CONTENTS

TABLE OF FIGURES

WHAT'S NEW IN THIS 2nd EDITION

The first edition of this book was published less than a year ago, in mid-December 2017. Things change so fast in self-publishing, though, that it's already time for a new edition and I ended up almost completely rewriting the original book. I'll just mention the biggest changes here.

Among many other changes, CreateSpace and Amazon KDP finally merged into a single platform. This was expected to happen sooner since Amazon acquired CreateSpace in 2005 and it brought welcome changes to Amazon KDP, such as expanded distribution of paperbacks.

Draft2Digital implemented some welcome changes too. They improved the design of their universal links and added new features to author pages, which made them even better than they already were. I also tested the Draft2Digital partner company Findaway Voices and have successfully published my first audiobook there.

The competition in self-publishing is growing fast and is becoming more and more challenging. I was shocked when I invested twice as much in promotion and sold three times as many copies of my third book than the previous one but couldn't even achieve the same overall rank on Amazon as I could a year ago with far fewer sales!

On the good note, the book *You Self-Publish, Now What? How to Promote Your Book* nevertheless became 1# New Release in several categories on Amazon while still on preorder. But, as said, the overall rank was still lower than expected and that means that the competition is fierce.

As for other changes, there have been upgrades of both MS Word and GIMP (a program I recommend for design and images). I thus updated the instructions and created all new print screens that will guide you through the tasks.

I also included a few additional resources in case that you are tempted to try the traditional route and get a publishing deal instead of self-publishing. I completely understand why this option might seem more and more alluring, but it's nevertheless far from easy and it certainly isn't fast.

WHO IS THIS BOOK FOR?

This book was written for those who would like to self-publish on a budget but cannot afford to invest much. It was also written for those who are cautious and want to test the waters before devoting a large budget to the endeavor.

Even though the book glances over all stages of the self-publishing process, it's focused mostly on technical aspects of it, such as paperback and ebook formatting, design, print, and distribution options. Technical aspects can be confusing, and these instructions will make them much easier for you.

You will also get formatting tips, recommended free tools for cover design, instructions on how to turn low-resolution pics into the 300 DPI needed for print and how to create a print-ready PDF. All of this is presented as a simple, step-by-step guide with pictures that show you exactly how to do it, so that you won't need to pay for any services.

Among other things, I also wrote this book to give you an idea of what it takes to self-publish and how much time, work, and money you'll need to put into it. You will also be able to estimate how much you can realistically expect to earn by selling your books.

NOTE:

You will have to install free software and have access to MS Word. If you don't have MS Word, the section on formatting might not be useful to you.

WHO AM I TO WRITE IT?

Like many before me, I started my writing career by trying to get a deal with a traditional publisher. It didn't take me long to realize that this was going to be a far bigger challenge than self-publishing. It's so much faster and easier to self-publish that I ended up doing that instead.

I successfully self-published my first three books using the tools and approaches described in this book. My ebooks [1] are available in all major online stores, the paperback editions and audiobook have been published on Amazon and are available through expanded distribution as well. The books have also received good reviews.

Most self-published writers suffer financial loss with their first book(s). By doing most of the work myself, I was able to avoid that to a significant degree but still had to pay for promotion, which did set me back. I wrote more on that in the second book in this series, *You Self-Published, Now What? How to Promote Your Book* [2].

Am I a best-selling author? Yes, my third book became #1 New Release and then also received a Best Seller label in several categories on Amazon. In terms of sales, however, we are talking about 170 copies sold on preorder. With the preorder price at $0.99 (that would be 35 cents in royalties) the Best Seller label didn't exactly make me rich.

Among other things, I wrote this book so that you can avoid scams and promises of huge self-publishing success if you only pay hundreds or even thousands of dollars for certain services. This book will help you self-publish at little or no cost and see what a beginner can realistically expect from self-publishing.

NOTE:

I am not affiliated with any of the products, platforms, and services recommended in this book. There are no affiliate links. The recommendations are based solely on my personal experience and satisfaction with these products and services.

1. INTRO TO SELF-PUBLISHING

Getting a deal with a traditional publisher is now close to impossible for most upcoming writers and even those who've made it are not always happy with what they got. Self-publishing makes the whole process a lot faster and easier. It also gives you full control over your book.

On the other hand, though, self-publishing also means that you will have to do everything yourself. Publishing a book may not sound that hard and it is indeed quite easy once you learn how to do it. But if you are doing this for the first time in your life, it will not be *that* easy – or at least not without guidance.

To-do list

If you want to do this right and come as close as possible to what a traditional publisher would do, you'll have to take care of everything on this most basic to-do list:

1. **Editing and proofreading**
2. **Illustrations and images (if any)**
3. **Book design**
4. **Cover design**
5. **Formatting for ebook and print edition**
6. **Distribution for ebooks and print editions**
7. **Bulk print or print-on-demand services**
8. **ISBN code**
9. **Author bio and blurb**
10. **Marketing and promotion**

Taking care of all this takes time and can cost a lot too. If you self-publish on a budget, you will have to do most if not all of the work yourself. You can also ask others to collaborate with you in return for a favor or credit in the book. Students, for instance, could use such collaborations as a work reference.

Start small

The best advice I can give you is to start small. Start by self-publishing a short story rather than a novel. That's how you'll become familiar with the process without too much pressure and frustration.

For a beginner, the amount of work can be daunting, even though this book will make it easier for you. Keep in mind that in traditional publishing this list would be taken care of by different departments and experienced professionals.

You have much to learn. When you do the formatting yourself, for instance, that alone can be nerve-wracking. That's why it would be best to start with a short story and fewer pages to deal with. Once you learn how to do it, it will be much easier to take on bigger projects.

Careful with online resources

Some of the blogs and websites are great and offer good advice to self-published writers. Unfortunately, though, there are also many that are selling associate links, products, or services that are unnecessary, overpriced, or of poor quality.

Make sure to check the list of best and worst self-publishing services by The Alliance of Independent Authors before paying for anything [3]. Many businesses make money by taking advantage of writers' dream to publish a book and don't care about what would be in the best interest of writers.

That's also why it might be a good idea to take your first book for a test drive and learn how to do everything yourself. Being familiar with all the stages of the process will help you identify and avoid shady services.

What if you'd get traditionally published instead?

Consider how hard it would be to get traditionally published. If you want to get published by one of the bigger publishing houses, you have to write in a popular genre and find an agent first. Getting an agent alone is quite a feat.

Read Jane Friedman's blog post "How to Find a Literary Agent for Your Book" to see how challenging that is [4]. Also, take a short quiz on Erica Verrillo's *Publishing... and Other Forms of Insanity* blog to find out if you are ready for an agent at all [5].

Even if you find an agent, that doesn't mean they will also get you a publishing deal. And if they do, this doesn't mean your book will become a success and won't flop miserably, which is what happened to Mark Dawson before he became a self-published superstar [6].

It might take years after you already finished a book before you find an agent and finally get it traditionally published. During that time, you could have already self-published several times instead of waiting for somebody else to take care of this.

Add to this full control over your book and higher royalties, and it's easy to see what makes self-publishing so attractive despite all the work it takes. Traditional publishing, however, might be a good option after you're already successful since you could get a much better deal.

2. SELF-PUBLISHING AS A BUSINESS

While this may sound disheartening and pessimistic, most first-time self-published writers end up generating a loss with their first book(s). There are many reasons for this.

Inexperienced writers, for instance, tend to overestimate their book's selling potential, have no following, fail to research the market and underestimate the need to invest in editing, book cover design, and promotion. This leads to unrealistically high expectations and loss.

Writing books and selling them are not one and the same thing. They are two different aspects of the publishing business and they require different sets of skills. Many writers feel that writing and self-publishing a book is easier than promoting and selling it.

Apart from the numbers that speak for themselves, there are several important differences between those self-published writers who make over $100,000 and those who make less than $500 per year. According to The Written Word Media survey, successful self-published writers spend twice as much time (28.6 hours per week) writing new books.

They also invest in professional editing (from $250 to $1000), book cover design (from $100 to over $500), marketing, and paid promotion. Importantly, most of them have been self-publishing for at least 3 years [7].

A vast majority of big earners self-publish in the most popular genres: romance and paranormal romance, fantasy, science fiction, and thriller lead the pack by far. But financial success is hardly ever found in genres such as literary fiction, children's books, horror, and non-fiction [8].

Out of 2,000 indie authors who disclosed their earnings in another survey, only 13% were able to make a living by self-publishing while 17% made no sales yet [9]. Most of the writers who are earning a living with self-publishing have published at least five books and usually a lot more.

Estimate your earnings

Let's say that you are going to start by self-publishing a short story. Now let's see how much you can make. The recommended price point for short stories, especially if they don't include illustrations, is around $0.99.

Amazon, which is where most book sales take place, will give you 35% royalties for ebooks priced at less than $2.99. This means that with $0.99 ebook you will get $0.35 from each sale. If you sell 200 copies, you'd earn $70 before tax.

It is estimated that self-published authors sell from 100 to 500 copies of their first book in the book's lifetime. This depends on the popularity of the genre, quality of the book, and investment in promotion.

Amazon and other self-publishing platforms in the U.S. also deduct 30% tax from the royalties of international writers unless their country has a treaty with the States. Fill out the tax form on the platform to see how much tax you'll have to pay. Amazon, for instance, deducts 5% tax from my royalties.

3. DISTRIBUTION & PRINT

Be careful with your choice of a distribution platform, for it can come at a cost to your budget, time, and nerves. Even though there are quite a few, I'd only recommend two to a beginner – Draft2Digital and Amazon KDP.

They are by far the easiest to use and offer high royalties too (except for the low-priced ebooks on Amazon). These two platforms are all you need to get your ebook into all major online stores as well as publish a paperback edition.

On Amazon KDP, you can also opt for expanded distribution of paperback to other vendors. As for ebooks, Draft2Digital distributes them to all major online stores, such as Apple and Kobo. You can also publish and distribute audiobooks through Draft2Digital's partner Findaway Voices.

What follows is a breakdown of the pros and cons for both platforms so that you'll know what to expect. Amazon KDP isn't perfect, and neither is Draft2Digital, but then no other self-publishing platform is.

Amazon KDP

One of the main benefits of Amazon KDP is that it is the fastest and cheapest option for publishing paperbacks and even more so for full-color print editions. This is a print-on-demand option, so there is no upfront cost since the book is only printed when somebody orders it. You can hardly beat the cost of shipping and printing on Amazon KDP, and the quality is pretty good too.

The platform recently merged with Create Space and thanks to this now also offers Expanded Distributing. This means the book will be available on sales channels other than

Amazon. This option, however, comes with extremely low royalties. Also, unknown writers stand little chance of selling many books on these channels [10].

Amazon KDP is currently in beta. The platform is thus a work in progress and there is a lot of experimenting going on. Because of that, not everything is always running smoothly and with no issues.

Amazon also tends to make unexpected changes, such as the removal of the 'Also Bought' section from product pages that has lately been a cause of much concern among readers and writers alike [11]. More than one writer reported a sharp drop in their sales following this change.

Paperback royalties

You may have heard that you will earn 60% royalties on paperback editions published on Amazon KDP. While this is indeed better than what other distribution platforms offer, it is not nearly as good as it sounds.

If you thought that the cost of print would be deducted from the selling price and you would get 60% from what remains, you are in for a nasty surprise. While Amazon indeed keeps 40% from the book's selling price, it then deducts the cost of print from your 60% royalties. This, in effect, leaves you with peanuts.

So how much will you earn in paperback royalties? It depends on how comfortable you feel with pushing the price of your book high, but whatever you do, you'll make nowhere near what Amazon is making.

KDP Select – yes or no?

Amazon KDP will try to convince you to enroll your ebook in KDP Select. This means that you won't be allowed to sell or offer your book for free anywhere else, including your website, for a minimum of 90 days. The exclusivity, however, only applies to ebook and not other editions of the book.

In return, Amazon will give you access to two promotional tools: Kindle Countdown Deal and Free Book Promotion. You will also get higher royalties for lower priced books in some markets (Japan, India, Brazil, and Mexico), and your ebook will become available through Kindle Unlimited so that you could earn additional royalties.

While this may sound enticing, I'm not a huge fan of it. There is more than one problem with this deal. For one, the promotion tools are limited to but a few days in each 90-day cycle so their effect on the book sales is limited too (more on that in the second book in this series, *You Self-Published, Now What? How to Promote Your Book*) [2].

My biggest concern with this option, however, is that Amazon is getting dangerously good at eradicating or acquiring its competitors. By luring authors in the exclusive 90-day deal, KDP Select hurts other ebook distributors and while this might lead to short-term benefits for the authors, it is not in their best interest in the long run.

A case in point, Amazon has recently destroyed self-publishing careers of several writers by banning them from the platform and withholding their royalties. While this might have been well-deserved in some cases since certain writers indeed gamed the system and took advantage of the loopholes in Kindle Unlimited, there were also those who said they were punished for no reason but could not appeal [12].

Pros – Amazon KDP

Despite the aforementioned issues, there are also plenty of pros when it comes to publishing on Amazon KDP:

1. **Your ebook and paperback will be available globally.** Having a paperback published on Amazon is pretty much all you need for a start.
2. **Expanded distribution.** You can select this option and have your paperback distributed to other vendors and libraries as well.
3. **Low print and shipping costs.** Amazon KDP is by far the most affordable option, especially for full-color print.
4. **Good paperback quality.** The quality is good for both, black & white as well as full-color print.
5. **Cover Creator and Book Cover Templates generator.** Creating a book cover for print can be tricky since you need to calculate the spine width and properly place the ISBN code. Amazon's Cover Creator and Book Cover Templates generator will take care of that for you.
6. **Free ISBN.** You won't need to buy ISBN for your book since Amazon gives you one for free.
7. **Fast and easy way to promote your book**. Amazon Advertising is integrated into Amazon KDP.
8. **High royalties, but only for a limited price range**. If you price your ebook at $2.99 or higher, but less than $9.99, you get 70% royalties.
9. **You can set a different price for the same book on different global markets**, and thus make it affordable across the markets.
10. **Free uploads for minor corrections.** Especially if you are doing this for the first time, errors might find a way into

your book. You can upload minor corrections free of charge even after the book was published.

11. **Book series option on product pages.** One of the welcome new features on Amazon is the ability to create a series and have all the books in the series displayed on each of the individual book's product pages. You'll have to contact Amazon KDP and ask them to enable this option, though.

12. **You can order proof and author paperback copies at a reduced price.** You'll only pay the price of print and shipping for these. Proof copies have a watermark on the cover and no ISBN code, but author copies are the same as the regular copies.

13. **You can put your book on permafree with Match Price.** To offer your book for free indefinitely, you'll have to set its price to zero on other platforms (Kobo, Apple…) first and then send the link to Amazon KDP support and ask them to match the price to zero.

Cons – Amazon KDP

On the other hand, though, here is the not-so-good part:

1. **Low royalties for ebooks priced at less than $2.99 or more than $9.99.** If your book is on a cheaper end, you will only receive 35% royalties.

2. **Low royalties for Expanded Distribution.** The minimum price for paperbacks distributed to other platforms is much higher than on Amazon while the royalties are significantly lower.

3. **Your ebook will only be available on Amazon.** Amazon KDP doesn't distribute ebooks to other stores, even though it distributes paperbacks widely.

4. **Cover Creator is not recommended for ebook covers.** There are far better tools available for ebook cover design, such as Snappa or Canva.

5. **If you enroll the book in Amazon KDP Select, you can only use the special promotion options for a limited time.** You also have to pick either the free ebook option (five days) or Kindle Countdown Deal (seven days).

6. **The ebook and paperback edition might not automatically link on Amazon's product page.** If that happens, you'll have to contact Amazon KDP customer service and ask them to link the book editions.

7. **Despite uploading an updated version of your paperback, Amazon might keep selling the old one.** This happened to me after I uploaded a new version with corrections. I ordered the paperback twice but kept receiving the old version. To their credit, Amazon KDP issued a full refund.

8. **Weird reasons for rejecting your paperback.** Amazon KDP rejected my paperback without explanation, so I had no idea what the problem was. It turned out that the book was rejected because someone mistook the chapter headings (Roman numerals) for page numbers. Sorting that out took days and the issue had to be escalated to the department manager.

9. **Customer service is getting worse.** The only option to contact customer service on Amazon KDP is through a contact form. It can thus take days or even weeks before the issues are resolved. In my experience, some of the representatives are completely incompetent. The worst case was when my fable was inexplicably categorized as horror by Amazon. It took weeks and numerous emails before I finally came across a representative who was able to take care of it.

10. **Amazon KDP deliberately edits paperback covers to look less nice than they really are.** The black paperback cover for my first book, for instance, is shiny and glossy because that is the kind of the finish I chose, but it looks gray, matte, and washed-out on Amazon. The weird explanation they gave me was that they adjust book cover images for paperbacks to make them look more 'realistic.'

11. **Limited preorder options.** You need to upload a full manuscript to set up a preorder. You can only create a preorder for no more than 90 days in advance.

12. **You cannot change the publishing date for preorders.** This will be an issue if you cannot publish the final version of the manuscript by the deadline. You can, however, cancel a preorder (better than risk getting poor reviews) but Amazon will punish you by preventing you from using this option again for a full year.

13. **Don't use your Amazon affiliate link to buy your own books.** Amazon might also suspend your affiliate account without warning even if your friends or family buy your books using your affiliate code.

14. **No PayPal payments.** If you need to receive your royalties through PayPal, Amazon KDP is not an option. (You can publish your ebooks on Amazon through Draft2Digital, though, and then get Amazon's royalties through PayPal, but they will be lower.)

15. **Audiobook option is only open to writers in selected countries.** Amazon KDP has a partnership with ACX, an audiobook platform that is only open to authors from the US, UK, Canada, and Ireland.

Bottomline

Amazon KDP is improving in some ways and getting worse in others. Despite obvious drawbacks and issues, however, the benefits (for now) still outweigh the downsides. The main problem with Amazon is that it has a monopoly in the self-publishing market.

This makes it uncomfortably easy for Amazon to destroy not only its competition but also careers of individual writers at a whim. One thus needs to be careful with going exclusive on Amazon. Having a plan B and distribution on other platforms is recommended.

Draft2Digital

Publishing ebooks with Draft2Digital is the fastest and easiest imaginable. The platform's mission is to make the whole process as frustration-free as possible and they've indeed managed to achieve it. Draft2Digital also offers quite a few useful tools, such as author landing page.

Pros – Draft2Digital

There is a long list of benefits when it comes to self-publishing with Draft2Digital:

1. **No complicated style/formatting guidelines.** What they have instead is a nice, short, and simple FAQ, and that's pretty much all you'll need.
2. **Fast and easy self-publishing for ebooks.** Draft2Digital is a highly intuitive and user-friendly ebook platform. All stages of publishing are a breeze.

3. **Distribution to all major online bookstores – iBooks, Barnes&Noble, Kobo, KoboPlus, Scribd, Tolino, 24 Symbols, Playster, and more.** They are constantly adding new ones, including distribution to libraries.
4. **High royalties.** Royalties on Draft2Digital are 60%, with the exception of distribution to Amazon in which case they are much lower.
5. **Free ISBN.** ISBN number isn't necessary for publishing ebooks, but it might come in handy on some book promotion sites.
6. **Different ebook design options.** You can choose between various genre-based book designs. Applying them only takes a click.
7. **Automatically created *Table of Contents*.** The *Table of Contents* is automatically created from the chapter titles.
8. **You can add front and back matter (such as *Dedication* and *About the Author* pages) on the platform.** You can thus only upload the story, and then add other parts as you go.
9. **Payments through PayPal.** You can choose to receive royalties through PayPal.
10. **You can offer your book for free.** There is no time limit or any other restrictions for free ebooks.
11. **You can set up your book for preorder even if the manuscript hasn't been finished yet.** You don't have to upload the manuscript or even the book cover to set up a preorder. You can do it for up to a year in advance.
12. **You can change the publishing date for preorders.** This is most useful if it turns out that you won't be able to finish the manuscript in time.
13. **You can set a different price for the same book on different global markets.** Like on Amazon, this can help you make your book more affordable on some markets.

14. **Books2Read universal links and author pages.** Draft2Digital's companion website Books2Read lets you share all the links to online stores where your book is available on a single URL (universal link). Books2Read also lets you create a great-looking author landing page where you can showcase your books, get followers, link to your social media accounts, and more.

15. **Audiobook publishing is open to all.** Draft2Digital works in partnership with Findaway Voices that publishes and distributes audiobooks. The distribution includes all major channels, including Amazon, and is open to international writers.

Cons – Draft2Digital

As for the downsides, they are far and few between:

1. **Low royalties for distribution to Amazon – if you publish your ebook on Amazon through Draft2Digital, your royalties will be lower than what you would get on Amazon KDP.** Instead of 35% (for books priced at less than $2.99), you will only receive 30%, and instead of 70% (for books priced at equal or above $2.99), you'll only get 60%.

2. **Amazon can reject your book.** You cannot publish pre-orders on Amazon though Draft2Digital. Amazon can also block the distribution of your book for several other highly elusive reasons, such as writing about a topic that has already been covered by many other writers.

3. **Customer service is unable to solve all issues.** Draft2Digital's representatives are helpful but they sometimes cannot resolve all issues. I, for instance, once received lower royalties from Apple than I should have

and there was no explanation from Apple and nothing Draft2Digital could do about it. This, however, seemed to be the problem on Apple's rather than Draft2Digital's side.

Bottomline

Draft2Digital is an excellent and beginner-friendly ebook self-publishing platform that comes with many useful tools and perks. The platform also helps international writers turn ebooks into audiobooks, which might be something worth considering at some point in your self-publishing career.

The only thing I don't recommend Draft2Digital for is the distribution to Amazon. You will get lower royalties, won't be able to set up your book for preorder on Amazon, and the book might be rejected for no clear reason.

4. ISBN NUMBER

ISBN code is used for tracking the information on the book's title, author(s), edition, publisher, format, and sales. You don't need it for ebooks but it's mandatory for print editions. Depending on the institutions issuing it, it can come with special requirements and cost quite a lot too.

When publishing paperback, one of the first questions you will run into on Amazon KDP is whether you have your own ISBN code or would prefer to use the free one offered by the platform. The short answer to this is – take the free one and don't waste any more time on it.

As is often the case, the advice you find online can be misleading or outright wrong. As an example, I read that writers should get their own ISBN since that would attribute the sales across different distribution channels to the same book and thus increase the book's overall sales rank.

While this might indeed be true in some cases, it won't work if you publish on print-on-demand platforms such as Amazon. I acquired my own ISBN for the paperback edition and first used it on Amazon KDP. When I wanted to use it again for the distribution of the same paperback on another print-on-demand platform, the code was rejected with the explanation that it had already been used.

The only reason why it might nevertheless be a good idea to get your own ISBN is if you are an international writer and would like to have your books cataloged in the national library in your home country. I was able to get the ISBN for my book from the national library for free, so this can sometimes be done at little or no additional cost.

5. EDITING AND PROOFREADING

Editing and proofreading are among those things that can ruin your book sales and reviews if you neglect them. At the very least, proofreading is essential, and it needs to be done by a human in addition to software.

Unfortunately, that's one thing you cannot do yourself because we tend to become blind to errors once we have seen the text too many times. This is also one of the reasons why I suggest you start small, with a short story rather than a novel.

If you hire someone to edit or proofread your book, they will charge per word – the shorter the book, the lower the cost. You can also ask a friend or a supporter for a favor, which is much easier if they only have to proofread a novella rather than a 100,000 words novel.

Try to polish the text as much as you can before handing it out for proofreading. The fees usually depend on how many errors there were and if you asked someone for a favor, you should also make their work as easy and not as hard as possible.

Using only a spell-checker in MS Word is not enough. At the very least, also run the text through proofreading apps, such as Grammarly, Hemingway Editor, or Pro Writing Aid. These apps will also give you suggestions on how to improve your writing and not just get rid of grammatical errors.

There are other free online resources available that are useful if you self-publish on a budget. You can, for instance, download a free *U.S. Government Publishing Office Style Manual* [13] and use it as a style guide.

Another useful resource is *The Punctuation Guide* [14], a free online tool where you can check punctuation based on

The Chicago Manual of Style and *The Associated Press Stylebook*. The former is used in the publishing industry, so use it as a reference when writing a book.

Another useful option is taking courses on grammar, style, and editing. You can find and audit these for free on platforms such as Coursera.

6. COVER DESIGN

As already stated, your book is a product, and you are launching it into a highly competitive market. Book cover design represents the all-important packaging of your product. Please refer to the next book in this series, *You Self-Published Now What, How to Promote Your Book* [12] for the in-depth explanation, but the key points of cover design are:

- **Make sure the cover stands out among other books** and draws attention to itself even at the smallest size (the size of the covers on Amazon)
- **The title should be easy to read even at a small size** and should give a clue as to what can the readers expect in terms of content
- **Style should fit the genre** – different genres call for different designs and images

Coming up with effective book cover design isn't easy. While it might be tempting to brush that aside and leave it for the last moment, that is not recommended since the cover is one of the key elements of the book. You will have to test different versions and ask your readers or fellow writers for feedback to come up with the best solution.

For the most competitive genres (romance, fantasy, YA, thriller…) it would be best to hire a professional designer or at least opt for a quality premade cover. For nonfiction, it's easier to create a cover yourself.

Ebook cover design

Creating a cover for ebook is technically far less demanding than for paperback. All you will need, to quote Draft2Digital's FAQ, is a tall rectangle in JPEG format. You can do that in Snappa or Canva, the recommended online apps for DIY ebook cover design.

These apps come with a nice selection of ebook cover templates and free fonts. An intuitive user interface gives you a limited range of design options, but it is easy to use and with a bit of effort you can create a decent cover there.

Another, but a lot more complex option with a rather steep learning curve is GIMP [15] – an open-source image manipulation program similar to Photoshop. GIMP allows you to create intricate designs with layers, so it might be worth the effort if you have the talent for it.

Paperback cover design

Everything that has to do with print is more complicated and paperback cover is no exception. While you only need the front cover for ebooks, paperback covers also includes the spine and back cover.

This means that you'll have to calculate the width of the spine based on the number of pages in your book, properly place the ISBN barcode on the back cover, and take the bleed into account as well. Luckily, *Amazon's Paperback Cover Template* and *Cover Creator* can help you with that.

Cover Creator

Amazon's Cover Creator is available through the *Bookshelf* in your KDP account. You will see this option when you start uploading and publishing your book. Cover Creator, though, is a rather crude and very basic tool and the templates are hideous. That's why I only recommend it for the last stages of the paperback cover design.

If you are going to use it, it's best to upload the front cover and then only create the spine and back cover there. This can work well enough for simple covers, especially nonfiction. The main benefit of Cover Creator is that it's fast and easy since it automatically takes care of the spine width, bleed, and ISBN barcode.

Amazon KDP Paperback Cover Template

Paperback Cover Template is a more complex option, but it lets you fully customize the cover. If you are going to hire a designer or buy a premade book cover, the designer will create the cover for you, but they will need a template with exact measures.

That's where Paperback Cover Template [16] comes in. You only have to select your book's size, insert the number of pages in the book, select paper color (yellow for fiction with no full-color illustrations, white for nonfiction), and download the template.

7. IMAGES

Any images in your book other than the book cover will significantly increase the cost of print. Not only is full-color print more expensive, you'll also have to use paper of higher quality needed for such print. You will thus have to raise the price of your book and that will affect the sales.

But images won't only add to the paperback costs, they will decrease your ebook royalties too. For ebooks priced at or above $2.99, Amazon charges delivery rates based on the file's size. You will be charged $0.15 per megabyte in the States, and similar rates apply in other territories as well [17].

Unless pictures are essential for your book or you are doing this more as an art project, it might thus be best to leave them out altogether or convert them to black & white.

Preparing images for publishing and print

One of the common reasons why your book or the cover could get rejected for print is image resolution. Any image you use in print edition, both inside the book and on the cover, must have a resolution of at least 300 DPI.

To check the resolution of your images and adjust it, you need an image manipulation program, such as Photoshop or GIMP [15]. To a writer on a budget, I recommend GIMP since it's free and will do the job well. It's also easy to use if you only want to adjust the resolution or resize an image.

If you used Canva or Snappa to create the cover, however, the image resolution will depend on the type of download you choose. In Canva, you'll be able to download the file as 'PDF-print,' which is exactly what you need to for Amazon KDP.

In Snappa, however, the only option of high-enough quality is 'retina PNG.' You'll then have to convert it to PDF using GIMP. To convert the file in GIMP, select 'Export as' option in the *File* menu, choose '*Select File Type by Extension,*' and select 'Portable Document Format' (pdf). Click 'Export' and you're done.

Ebook image size, type, mode & resolution

For a start, you need to know the exact size of the images you'll use. The recommended size for ebook cover on Amazon KDP is 1600 x 2560 pixels and 1600 x 2400 on Draft2Digital. You can, however, also use the same size on both platforms.

The recommended sizes for the images inside ebooks range from 600 x 450 for small to 1200 x 1800 pixels for full-page images. Amazon guidelines recommend the image resolution of 300 DPI even for ebooks. Many designers, however, agree that this isn't such a good idea. In the case of print screens (such as the ones used in this book), this would even make the images look worse.

You can try setting the resolution to 72 DPI, which is, in general, a recommended resolution for online use [18]. Many computer monitors, however, display images at 96 DPI, so 96 DPI might be another option [19]. In any case, check the converted ebook file to make sure the images look good before you publish.

Amazon's recommended format for ebook images is JPEG, but if you use Draft2Digital to convert the file into ebook, PNG might look better. Images should also be in RGB mode. RGB mode is a default mode in Canva, Snappa, and GIMP, so you don't have to worry about that. If you want to nevertheless check the mode in GIMP, open the image, select *Image* on the menu, and click *Mode* (see *Figure 1*).

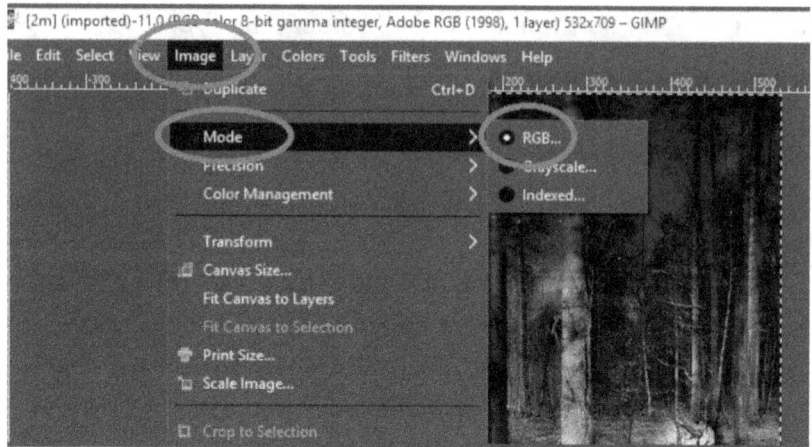

Figure 1 – RGB mode in GIMP

Paperback image size & resolution

For print, you need to know the exact sizes of the images in your book before adjusting the resolution. For the cover, this will depend on whether you are going to use the paperback cover template or Amazon's Cover Creator.

If you are going to use the Cover Creator, take the same front cover image as for the ebook, resize it to the size of your paperback (e.g. 6 x 9 inches), and adjust the resolution if needed. You'll learn how to do that later in this chapter. Upload that as your paperback's front cover and create the rest of the cover there.

In case that you are going to use Amazon's template and create the full cover (front, spine, and back) yourself, however, the image size will include all parts of the cover and Amazon KDP's Paperback Cover Template will calculate the exact size you need [16].

If you plan on using images inside your book as well, you will have to look up their sizes in the book's print-ready MS Word file. To insert an image in Word, place the cursor to where you want the image to be, select *Insert* tab from the main menu, and choose *Pictures* (see *Figure 2*). Click the image and drag its corner if you need to resize it. Place it as you want it to be in the book.

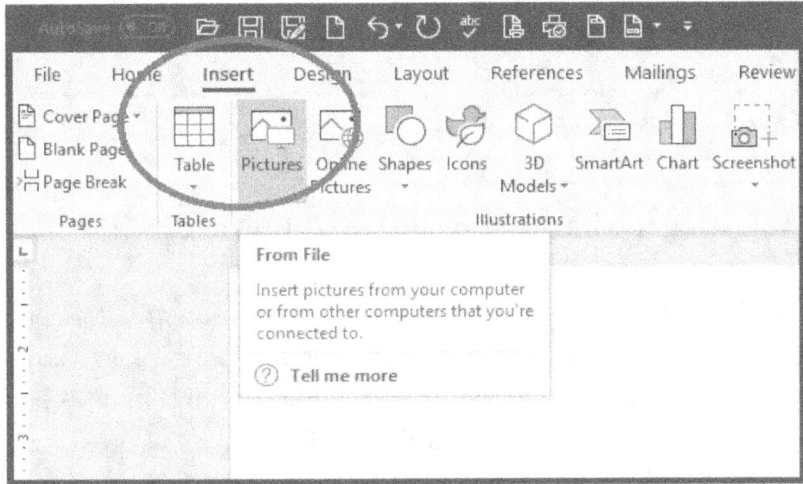

Figure 2 – Inserting image in MS Word

Then look up the image's size by double-clicking it. This will open *Picture Tools.* Click the *Format* tab and you will see the image size on the right side of the menu (see *Figure 3*). Use this size when adjusting the resolution in GIMP and then replace the placeholder image with the one you prepared for print. If the original image is smaller than what you need for print, you can also scale and enlarge it in GIMP.

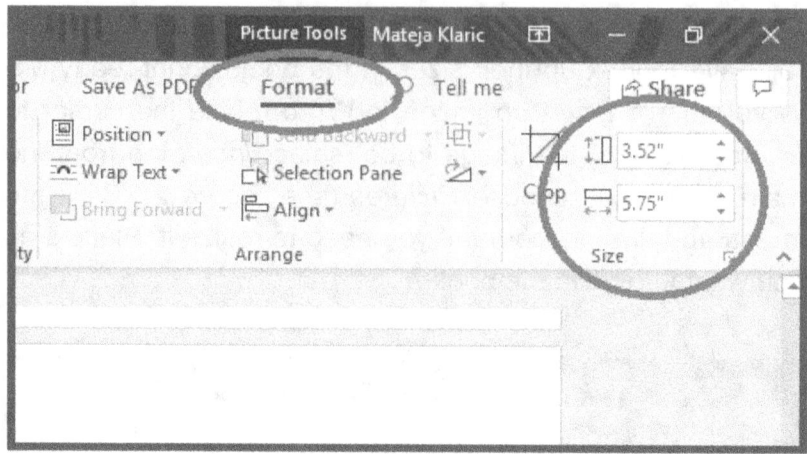

Figure 3 – Image size in MS Word

Adjusting the image size and resolution in GIMP

To change the size and image resolution, launch GIMP and open the image by going to *File > Open* on the main menu. Once the image is uploaded, click *Image* on the main menu and select *Scale Image* (see *Figure 4*).

This will open a dialog box with size and resolution options. Select the units you are using in MS Word – in this case, inches (see *Figure 5*). Set X and Y resolution to at least 300 pixels/in and click *Scale* (see *Figure 6*).

The image is now in high-resolution but in GIMP's XCF format. To use it in your MS Word file, you will need to export it as JPEG. Click *File* on the main menu and choose *Export* from the drop-down menu (see *Figure 7*).

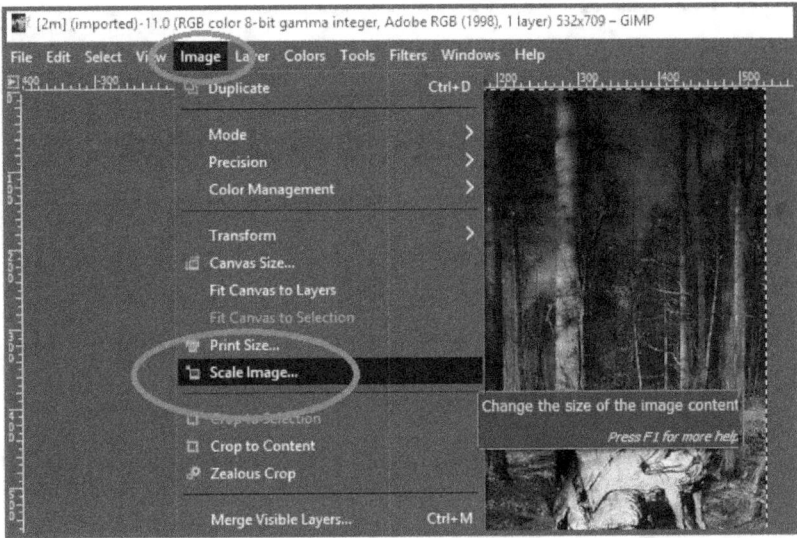

Figure 4 – Scaling image in GIMP

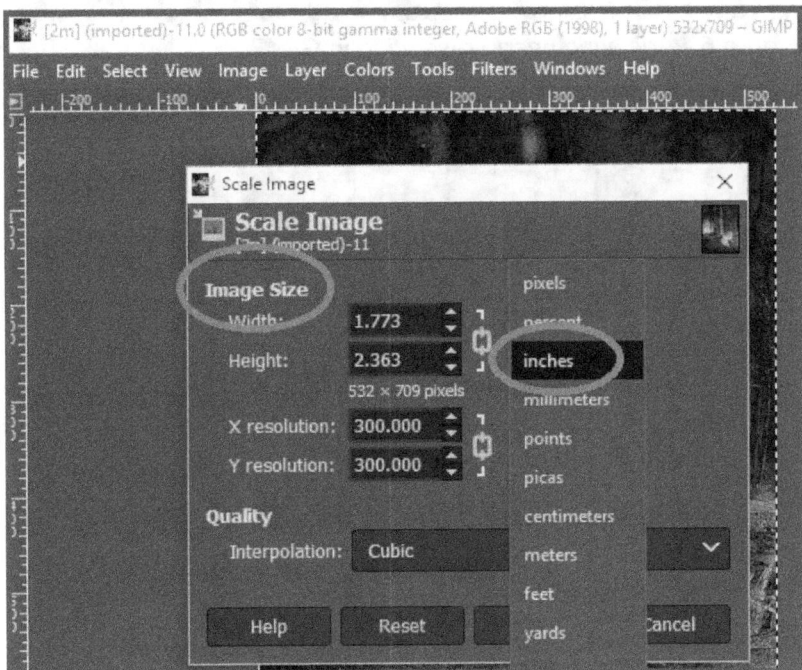

Figure 5 – Changing image size in GIMP

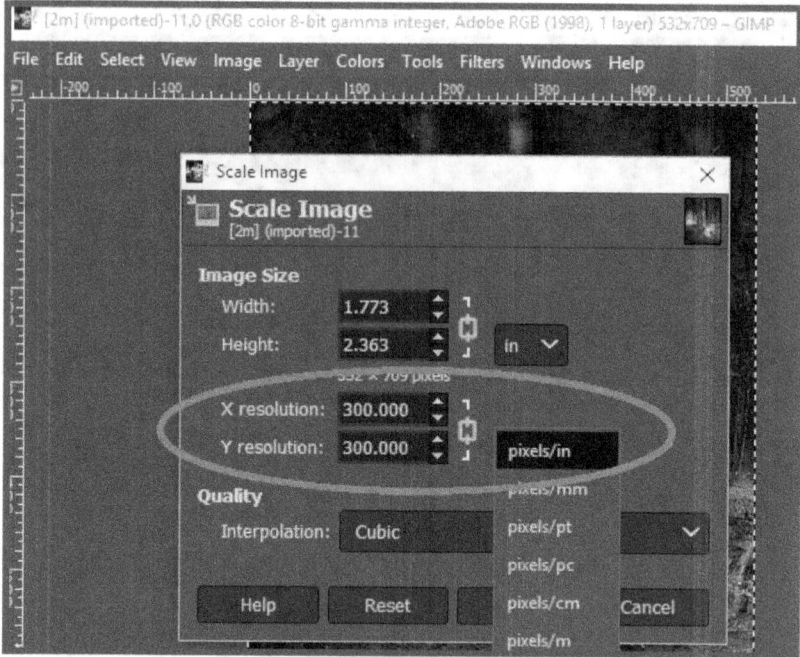

Figure 6 - Adjusting image resolution in GIMP

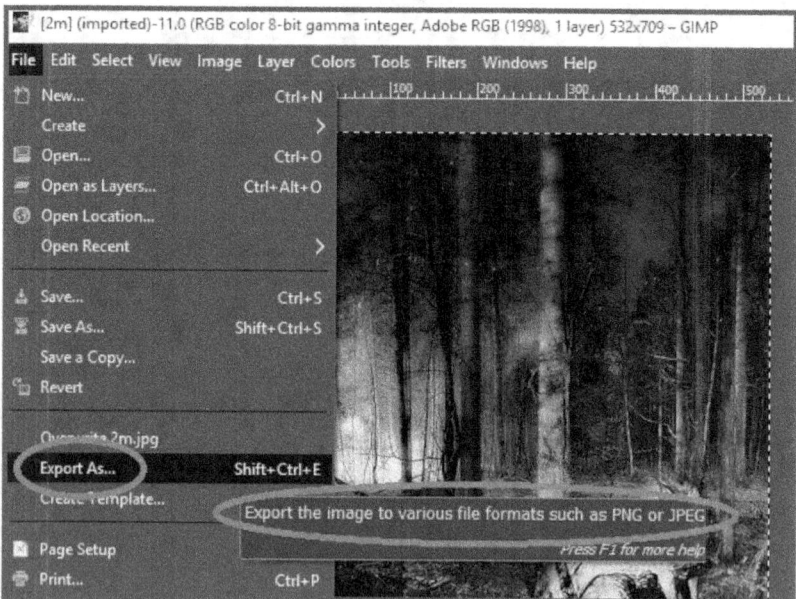

Figure 7 – Exporting image in GIMP

The *Export* option will open a pop-up window where you can save the image and select the format. Choose where to save the image first and then go to *Select the File Type (By Extension)* at the bottom of the window. Scroll down to find *JPEG Image*, select it and click *Export* (see *Figure 8*).

This will open a new pop-up window. Set quality to 100% and click *Export* again (see *Figure 9*). Now you can insert the image into your formatted MS Word book file or upload it to Amazon KDP Cover Creator as a book cover.

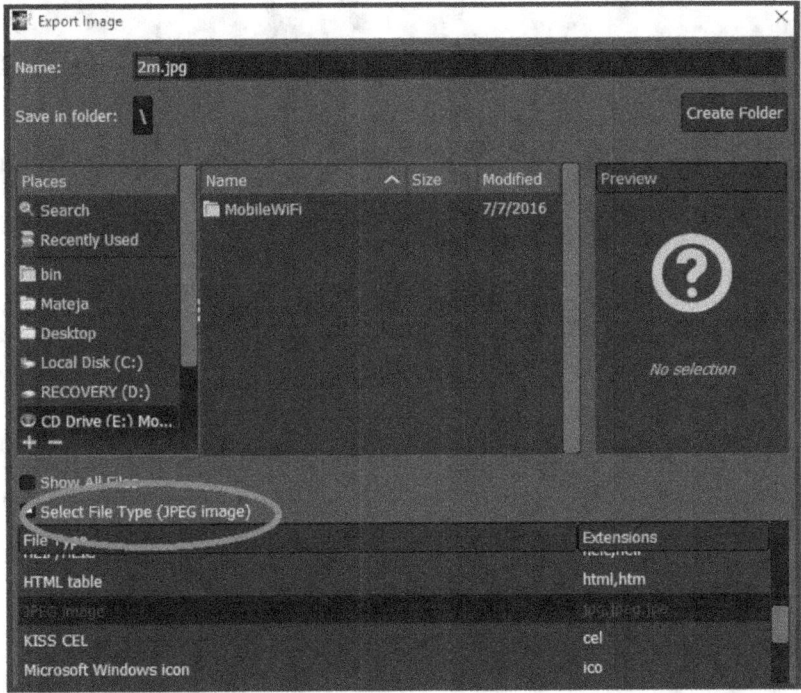

Figure 8 – Creating JPEG in GIMP

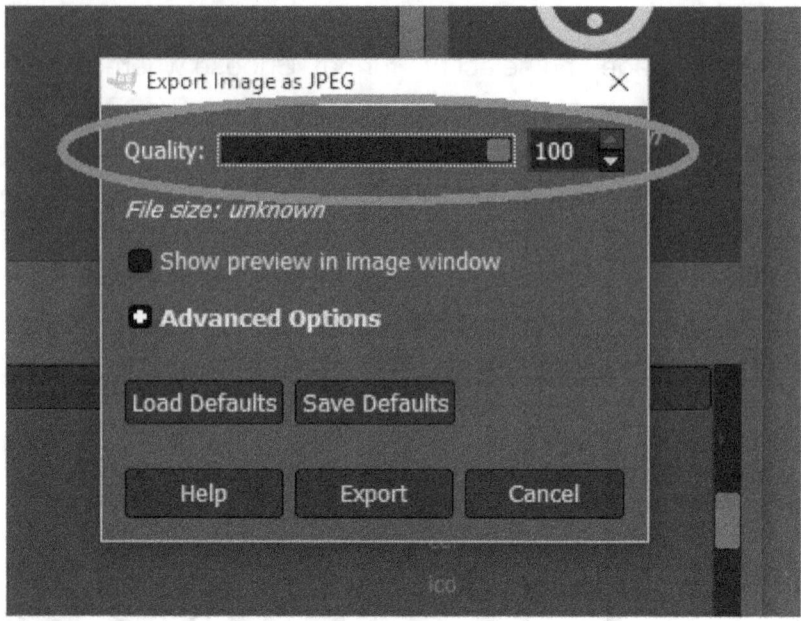

Figure 9 – Setting image quality in GIMP

Convert color images to black & white

You can also use GIMP to convert color images to black & white and thus reduce the cost of printing. To do that, click *Image* on the main menu and select *Mode*. Choose *Grayscale* (see *Figure 10*).

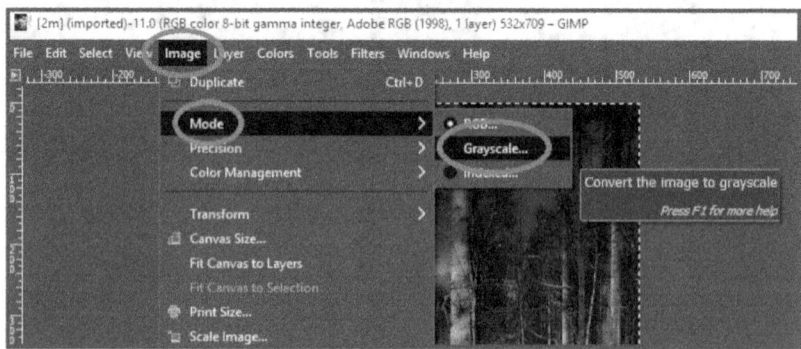

Figure 10 – Converting image to B&W in GIMP

Prevent MS Word from compressing the images

Even though you have all the images in MS Word in high resolution, Word will compress them by default and thus decrease their resolution. To prevent that from happening, click *File* on the main menu and scroll all the way down on the left menu to *Options*. Click it and select *Advanced*. Scroll down to *Image Size and Quality*. Select *Do not compress images in file* and click *OK* (see *Figure 11*).

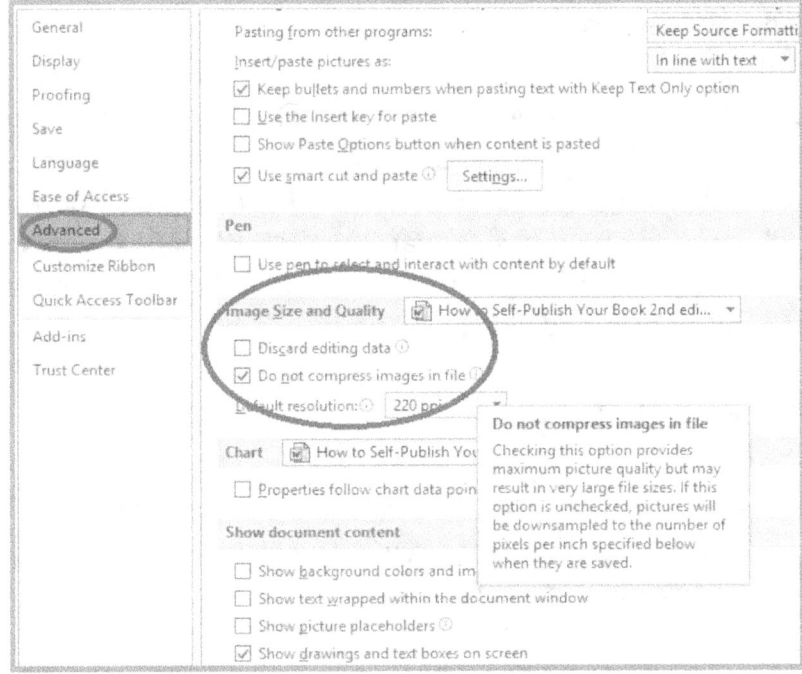

Figure 11 – Compressing images in MS Word

8. BOOK DESIGN

There are differences between ebooks and paperbacks when it comes to book design too. Designing an ebook is much easier because the layout depends on the device while fonts and spacing are a matter of personal choice of the reader. You can, however, design the print edition exactly as you want it to be.

Ebook design

Draft2Digital makes designing an ebook a breeze. After you upload the file, you'll be able to choose between various premade design options suitable for different genres. You will only need to do a basic formatting in MS Word first (how to do this will be explained in the next chapter), upload the file to Draft2Digital, and pick the design.

Paperback design

Paperback design and formatting are a lot more complex, but you can also get more creative with layout, fonts, and images. A few basic rules, however, apply:

- **Form follows function** – the main purpose of fonts is to make the book easy to read and not to make it look nice at the expense of readability.
- **Less is more** – keeping it simple usually works best.
- **Design should fit the genre** (romance and nonfiction, for instance, require different book design).

Fonts

When choosing fonts, the safest and easiest way would be to go with the ones that are most commonly used in publishing. You can easily find recommendations online, but many of these are professional fonts you would have to buy, and they are not exactly cheap.

You can, however, always use the most reliable and reader-friendly fonts you already have on your computer – Times New Roman for fiction and Arial for nonfiction. Another option is to download free fonts from Google Fonts [20].

Be aware, though, that while many fonts look good, not all are great for reading longer texts and not all will be readable at smaller sizes needed for books (from 10 to 12 point, depending on the typeface).

MS Word design styles

Especially for nonfiction, applying one of the MS Word styles can be a fast and easy solution to designing your paperback with one click. To use this option, click *Design* on the main menu and you will see different style options. Place the cursor on any of them without clicking and they will be applied to your document as a preview.

Additional design elements

You can also try placing vignettes (inserting them as images) at the beginning of chapters. Using drop caps is another simple and efficient way of making your book look nice.

To create drop caps in MS Word, select the first character in the opening paragraph and then go to *Insert* tab. You will find *Drop Cap* option in the *Text* section on the right. Click it and select *Dropped*. You can choose the size and font by clicking *Drop Cap Options* in the same menu (see *Figure 12*).

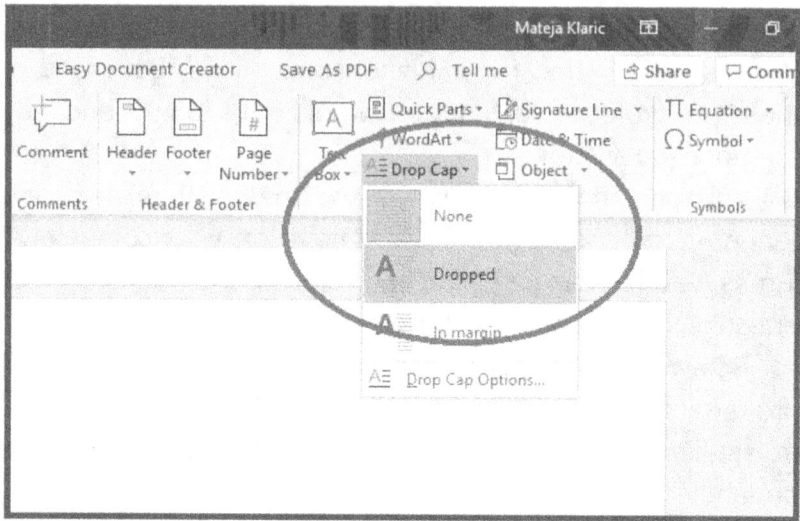

Figure 12 – Creating drop caps in MS Word

9. BOOK FORMATTING

You will need to format your MS Word book file in two different versions – one for ebook and another for paperback. Ebook formatting is very simple but paperback will again take more time and effort. You can also start with ebook and then create the paperback version from it.

Parts of the book

Books are divided into three main sections—in addition to the main one (the story itself), you will also have to create the front and back matter.

Front matter

Front matter is a mandatory part of every book. It is placed at the beginning of books and includes the following:

- **Title page** (twice for print editions)
- **Copyright page** (including the ISBN number)
- **Dedication** (if any)
- **Table of Contents** (paperback only)
- **Preface** (if any)
- **Introduction** (if any)

Back matter

Although it can be omitted, back matter is important. You can create additional pages at the end of the book to promote your other books, add a short bio, and include the links to your website or blog. You can also invite the readers to subscribe to your newsletter (please refer to book 2 in this series for more ideas and detailed instruction on how to do this [2]).

Ebook formatting

Start formatting your book by marking all chapter titles as *Heading 1*. Place the cursor next to each chapter title and click *Heading 1* in the *Home* menu (see *Figure 13*).

Next, insert page breaks between each chapter and between each section of the front and back matter. To do that, place the cursor at the end of the chapter or section, click *Insert* tab on the main menu, and select *Page Break* (see *Figure 14*).

With ebook formatting, things can be a bit unpredictable. You will have to check every page of the converted ebook files to make sure everything looks as it is supposed to. Unintentional double-spacing or change in fonts could appear in some paragraphs.

Use the *Show/Hide* button (¶) when formatting – you will find it on the *Home* menu next to *Styles* (see *Figure 15*). This will show underlying formatting and make it easier to locate errors. If you see errors in the converted files, you'll have to correct them in Word before uploading the file again.

If you cannot find the error or have issues you cannot resolve, highlight the problematic parts of the text and use *Clear Formatting*. You will find this command (the rubber symbol) on the *Home* menu in the *Font* section.

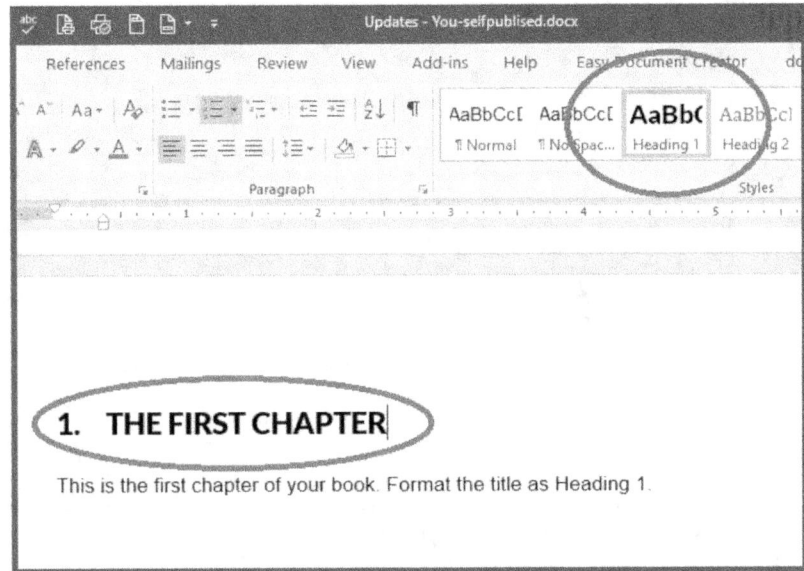

Figure 13 – Formatting chapter titles in MS Word

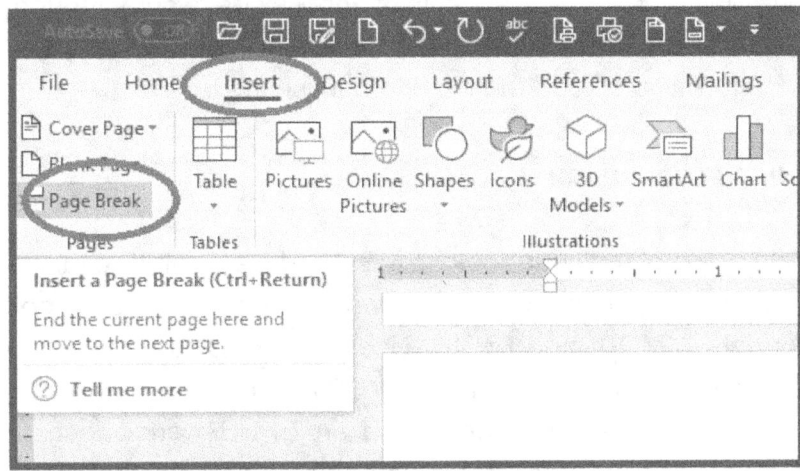

Figure 14 – Inserting page breaks in MS Word

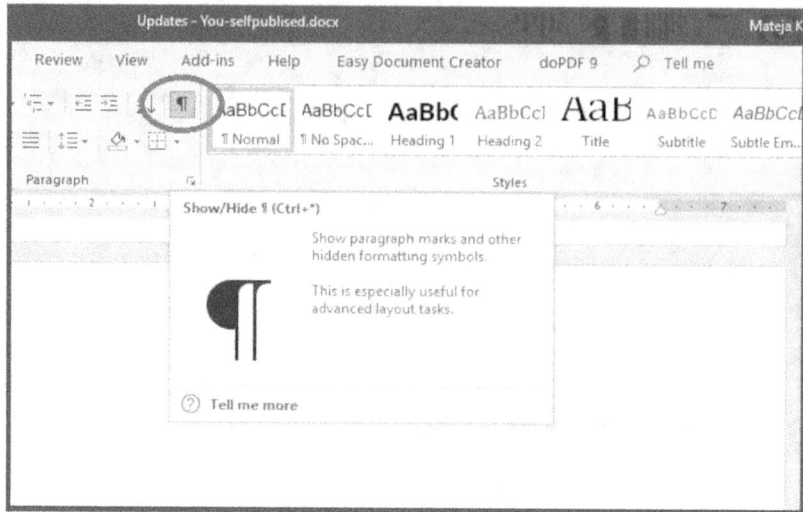

Figure 15 – Show/Hide button in MS Word

Finally, insert and check the links. The ability to add links is one of the most useful aspects of ebooks. Make sure, though, that they are functional and lead to where they are supposed to before you upload the file and publish it.

Ebook conversion

After you upload your book as MS Word file, Draft2Digital will automatically convert it into two commonly used ebook formats – MOBI and EPUB. Use this EPUB to upload and publish your ebook on Amazon KDP as well.

In my experience, uploading an EPUB works best on Amazon KDP – at least this was the only format that didn't lead to formatting issues with my ebooks. Draft2Digital also converts your file into PDF, but I do not recommend using that for paperback edition since the formatting is lacking.

Paperback formatting in MS Word

Paperback formatting in Word can be frustrating when it comes to section breaks, gutter, and images. There are also bugs in the latest versions of MS Word (Office 365) that cause problems with section formatting. This chapter will help you avoid most of these issues and show you how to export formatted MS Word file as the print-ready PDF you need for paperback editions.

Begin by setting the size of the document to the size of your paperback edition. You can do that in the *Layout* tab on the main menu. You will find *Size* option in the *Page Setup* section. Click *More Paper Sizes* to set up your custom size. Then proceed with the main sections – front matter, the story, and back matter.

Front matter in paperback

Before you start formatting the front matter, grab a couple of traditionally published paperbacks and check how that is usually set up. Not every paperback uses the same layout, but you will notice that there are certain rules they all follow. This section will guide you through them.

Title page

The title usually appears twice in traditionally published paperbacks in the States (in other parts of the world, the rules might be different). There is the book's title on the very first page of the book (facing the cover) where you often see only the title but no other information.

On the following pages, the title page appears again and includes all the information, such as the subtitle and author's name. The main title page is usually located before or next to the copyright page and always placed on the right side of the book.

Copyright page

Amazon KDP is extremely laid back when it comes to traditional publishing rules and the copyright page is not even a requirement when you self-publish there. Adding a copyright page, however, is advisable if you wish to have your rights legally protected as the author of the book.

Also, use the copyright page to give credit and protect the rights of everyone else who also contributed to the book with their art or services, such as illustrations, editing, and proofreading.

Table of Contents

With most genres, you will need to include the *Table of Contents* in print editions of the book. If you follow my advice and start self-publishing with a short story, however, that won't be necessary. Otherwise, MS Word can automatically create one and that's not too complicated.

You'll have to format all chapter titles as Heading 1 and subtitles as Heading 2 first. You've already done this when formatting the ebook but if you haven't yet, go to *Home* tab, click the title or subheading, and select *Heading 1* for chapter titles and *Heading 2* for subtitles (see *Figure 13*).

When done, place the cursor on the page where you would like to have the *Table of Contents*, click *References* on the main menu, and select *Table of Contents*. You will find it on the left side of the menu. This will open three different options you can choose from (see *Figure 16*). Selecting the first or second one will automatically create *Table of Contents* for your book.

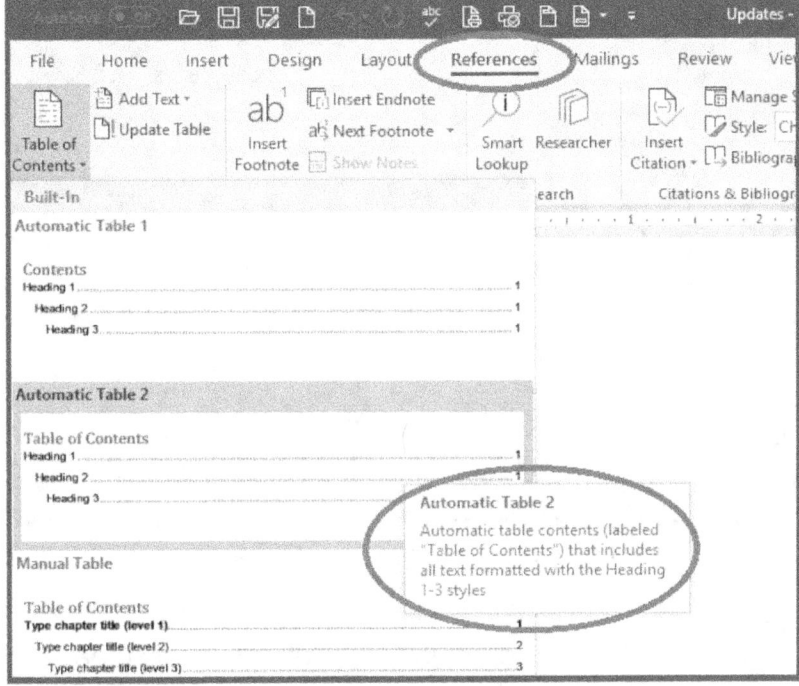

Figure 16 – Creating Table of Contents in MS Word

You can also customize the table by selecting *Custom Table of Contents* from the dropdown menu (see *Figure 17*). If you choose that option, you'll be able to select the number of levels shown (e.g. only chapter titles and no subtitles) and change the style.

Automatic Table 2

Table of Contents

Heading 1 1

Heading 2 1

Heading 3 1

Manual Table

Table of Contents

Type chapter title (level 1) 1

Type chapter title (level 2) 2

Type chapter title (level 3) 3

Type chapter title (level 1) 4

More Tables of Contents from Office.com ▶

Custom Table of Contents...

Remove Table of Contents

Figure 17 – Custom Table of Contents in MS Word

If you make any changes in the book later, you'll have to manually update the table. To do this, click on the table, go to the *References* tab and choose *Update Table.*

This will open a dialog box with additional options. Choose *Update page numbers only* if you only added or removed parts of the text and *Update entire table* if you added or changed subtitles or chapter titles.

Table of Figures

Especially if you publish nonfiction, your book might include images as well. If that is the case, you can also include the *Table of Figures.*

Creating *Table of Figures* takes a bit more work since you'll have to add a caption to each image first. To add a caption, click the image, go to *References* on the main menu, and select Insert Caption (see *Figure 18*).

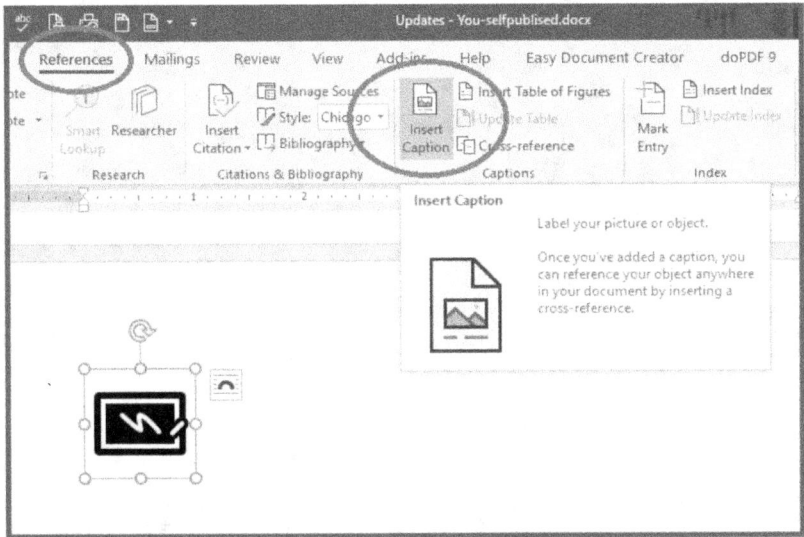

Figure 18 – Inserting image caption in MS Word

Once you added captions to the images, click on to the page where you'd like to have the *Table of Figures*, select *References* on the main menu, and click *Insert Table of Figures* (see *Figure 19*).

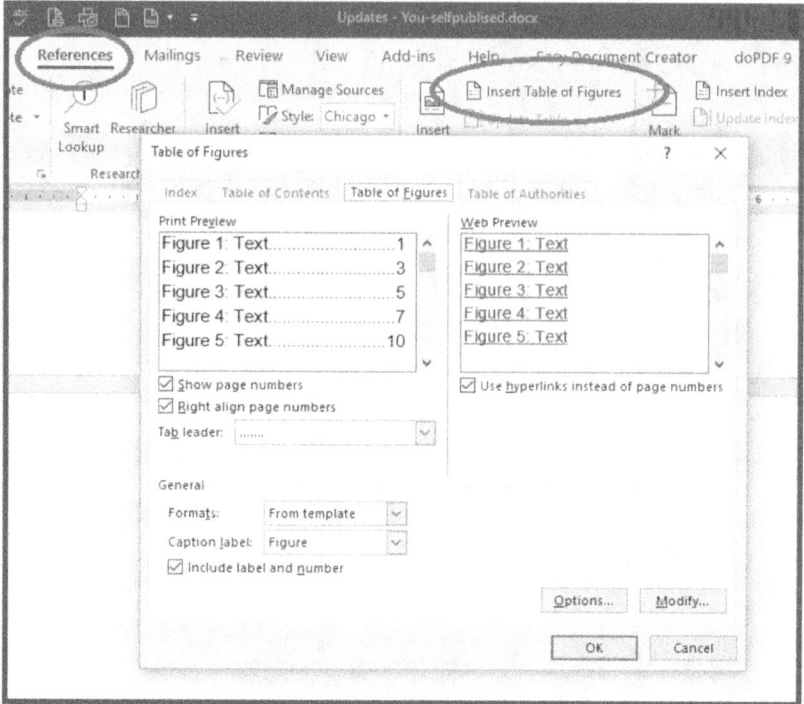

Figure 19 – Creating Table of Figures in MS Word

Create sections in paperback

When formatting the front matter, the story, and back matter you'll have to add *Section Breaks* between each of these parts. This is necessary because section breaks let you format these parts of the document separately.

It's best to use the *Show/Hide ¶* button (see *Figure 15*) while working on this since it will make section breaks visible. Create the first section break by placing the cursor at the end of the front matter. Click the *Layout* tab on the main menu, select *Breaks*, and scroll to *Section Breaks* (see *Figure 20*).

Choose the *Next Page* option, so that the new section starts with the first chapter of the book. If you also added back matter, repeat this either at the end of the last chapter or after the references if you included those too. You can now apply different formatting to each of the sections.

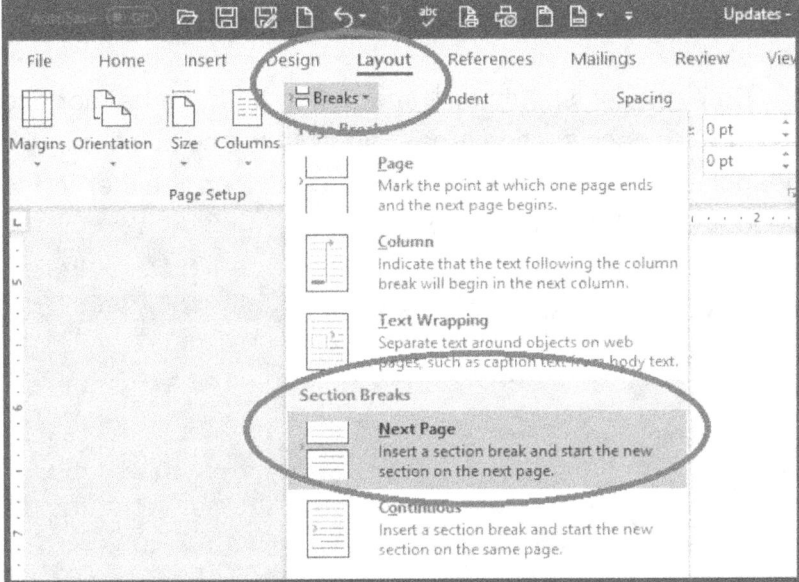

Figure 20 – Inserting Section Breaks in MS Word

Format header and footer

Print editions have the title in the header and pagination only in the footer or header of the story, but not in front and back matter. Go to the story part and open the header. You can do this either by double-clicking on the top of the page or by clicking *Insert* tab on the main menu and selecting *Header*.

There are some issues that could pop-up while you're adding content to header and footer. For one, you need to make sure that you don't have the *Link to Previous* option selected. If you do, everything you'll put in the header or footer of one section will be automatically applied to the previous section as well. That's not what you want.

Click *Link to Previous* on the menu dashboard and make sure it's turned off (see *Figure 21*). Also, you don't want the *Different First Page* option selected (in the same menu) since you need to apply the same header and footer to all pages in the story section.

Both options should be turned off in both the header and footer after each section break. Now put the book's title in the header. As for the pagination, you can insert it either in the header or footer (see *Figure 22*).

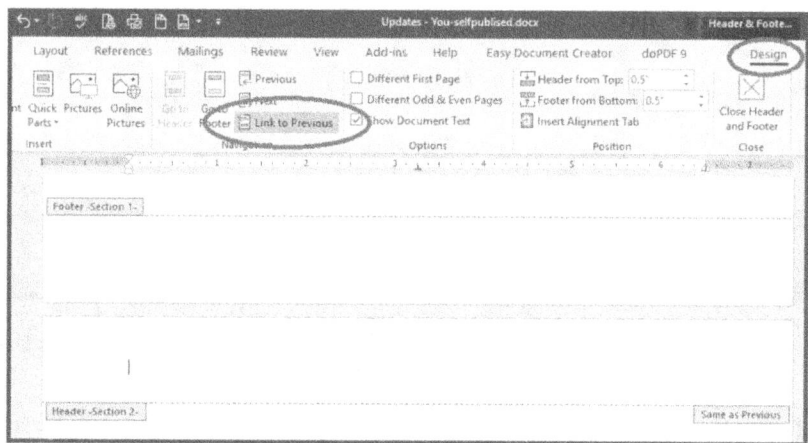

Figure 21 – "Link to Previous" in MS Words

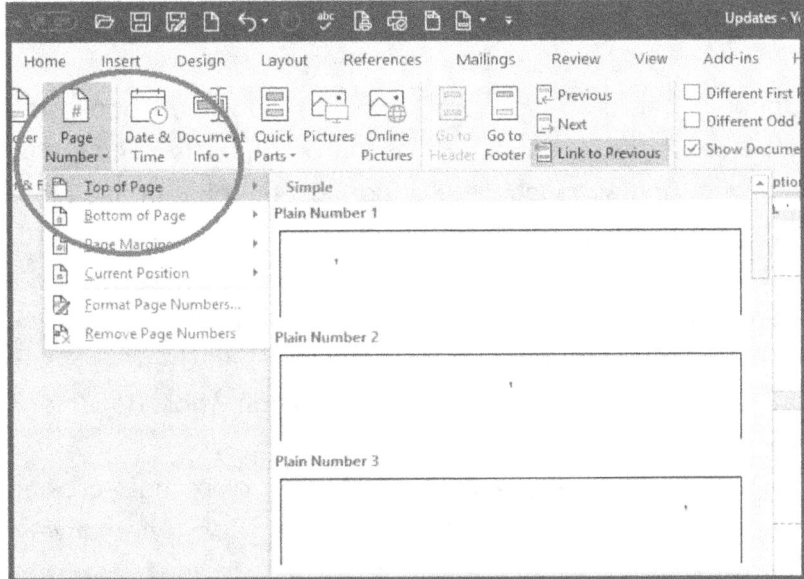

Figure 22 - Adding page numbers in MS Word

Justify the text

Unless you publish poetry or picture books, text in books is justified, so that it's evenly aligned to both margins. You can align the text by using *Select All* command (CTRT+A) and then clicking *Justify* option in the *Paragraph* section of the *Home* menu (see *Figure 23*).

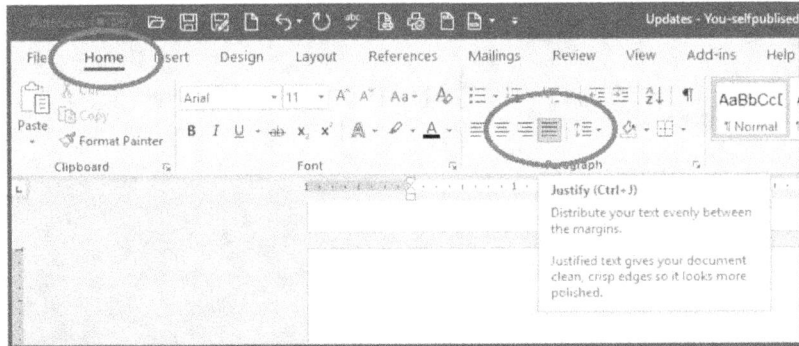

Figure 23 - Justifying the text in MS Word

Paragraphs indentation

Opening paragraphs in professionally published books are not indented. This goes for the first paragraphs in chapters, sections, and subsections. For nonfiction, you can use block paragraphs instead of indentation.

If you'll use indentation, don't do it with *Tab* key but set it manually instead. The recommended size is about the same as the height of the font. This is usually somewhere between 0.2" and 0.25". To set the indentation for the whole document, use *Select All* command (CTRL + A).

You can then adjust it using the ruler or by right-clicking the highlighted text and choosing *Paragraph.* Alternatively, you can also click the small arrow next to the *Paragraph* section in the *Home* menu (see *Figure 24*). The latter two options will open a pop-up window.

In this pop-up window, go to *Special*, select *First Line* from the options and set it to the desired size. Don't forget to then also manually set the opening paragraphs back to no indentation using the ruler (see *Figure 25*).

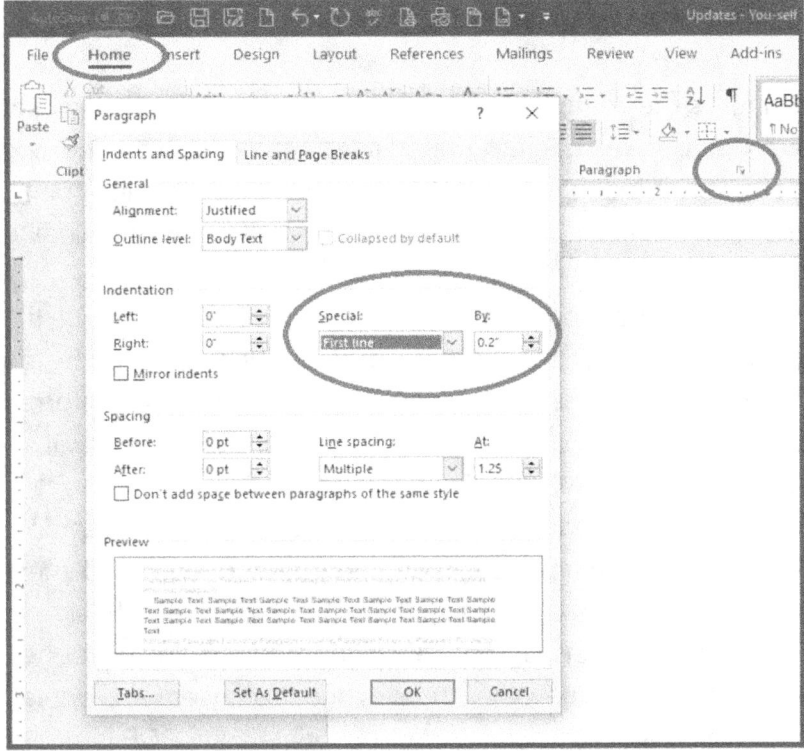

Figure 24 – Setting the indentation in MS Word

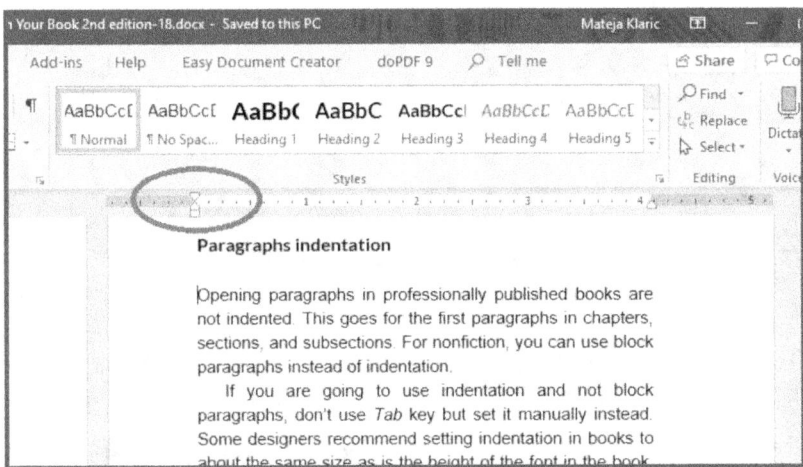

Figure 25 – Opening paragraphs in MS Word

Setting the gutter and margins

Gutter is the margin closest to the book's spine. The thicker the book, the wider the gutter needs to be so that the text doesn't get eaten up by the spine. Even with thinner books, though, it doesn't hurt to account for the fact that the binding will eat up some of the page.

Check Amazon KDP's guidelines since the size of the gutter and margins depend on the number of pages in the book (See *Figure 26*). Be aware though, that what is referred to as *Inside Margins* in the Amazon KDP guidelines will, in fact, be *Outside Margins* in your Word document.

This is so because Word doesn't take the book cover into account and thus processes the first page of your document as the page that would be on the left and not the right side of the book. The first page of your print-ready file, however, will be on the right side of the book since the covers are printed separately and are not a part of the print-ready PDF file.

Page Count	Inside (Gutter) Margins	Outside Margins (no bleed)
24 to 150 pages	0.375" (9.6 mm)	at least 0.25" (6.4 mm)
151 to 300 pages	0.5" (12.7 mm)	at least 0.25" (6.4 mm)
301 to 500 pages	0.625" (15.9 mm)	at least 0.25" (6.4 mm)
501 to 700 pages	0.75" (19.1 mm)	at least 0.25" (6.4 mm)
701 to 828 pages	0.875" (22.3 mm)	at least 0.25" (6.4 mm)

Figure 26 - Gutter and margins on Amazon KDP

To adjust the gutter, go to the *Layout* tab on the main menu, click *Margins*, and then click *Custom Margins* at the bottom of the dropdown menu (see *Figure 27*). This will open a pop-up window with various options.

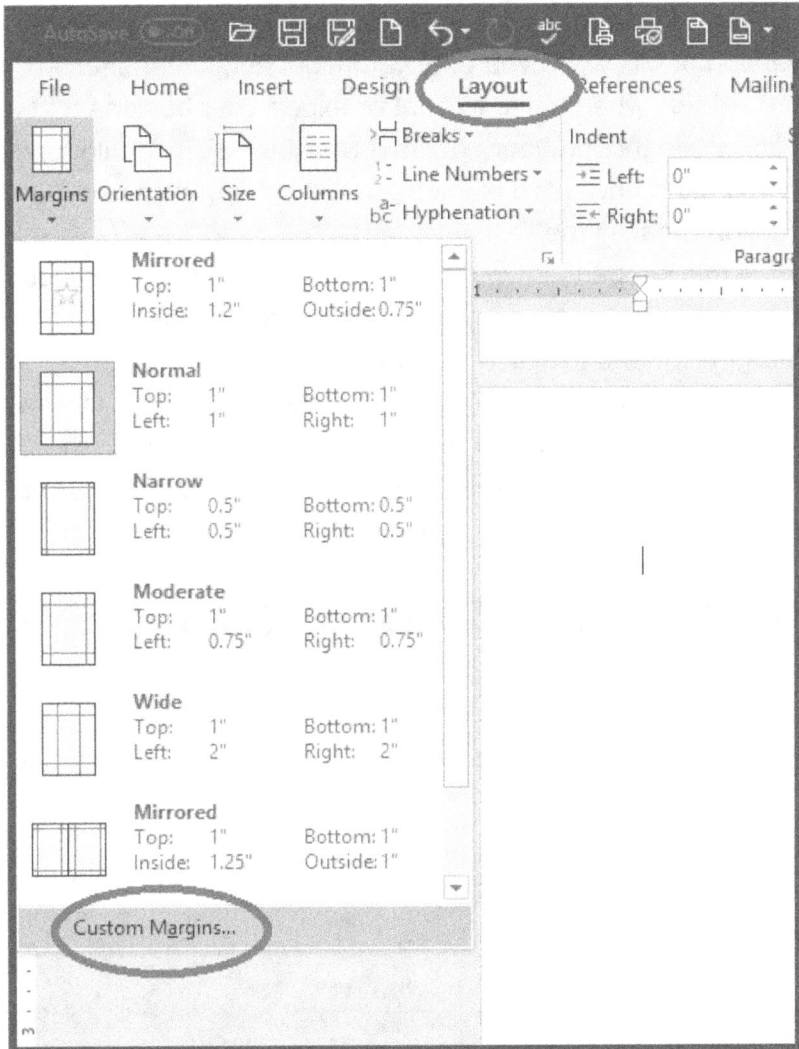

Figure 27 – Gutter and margins in MS Word

Due to the before mentioned reason, don't use the *Gutter* option, for it will place the gutter on the wrong side of the page. Use *Mirror margins* instead (see *Figure 28*). You need to set the *Outside* margin as the gutter (see *Figure 28*).

As already mentioned, there is a bug in some of the MS Words versions and it disrupts section breaks when you convert MS Word file into PDF file. Depending on which version of MS Word you use, you might encounter section break bugs when trying to print or export your book as a PDF. Even though your document will look as it should have in Word, an unwanted blank page will appear after each section break in the PDF.

If this happens to you, it will mess up the gutter settings in your PDF. In that case, you will have to set up the margins for each section separately to account for the unwanted blank pages. What you need to achieve is to have the gutter on the left side of the first page and then on the right side of the next page. This has to alternate in that order throughout the book with no exceptions.

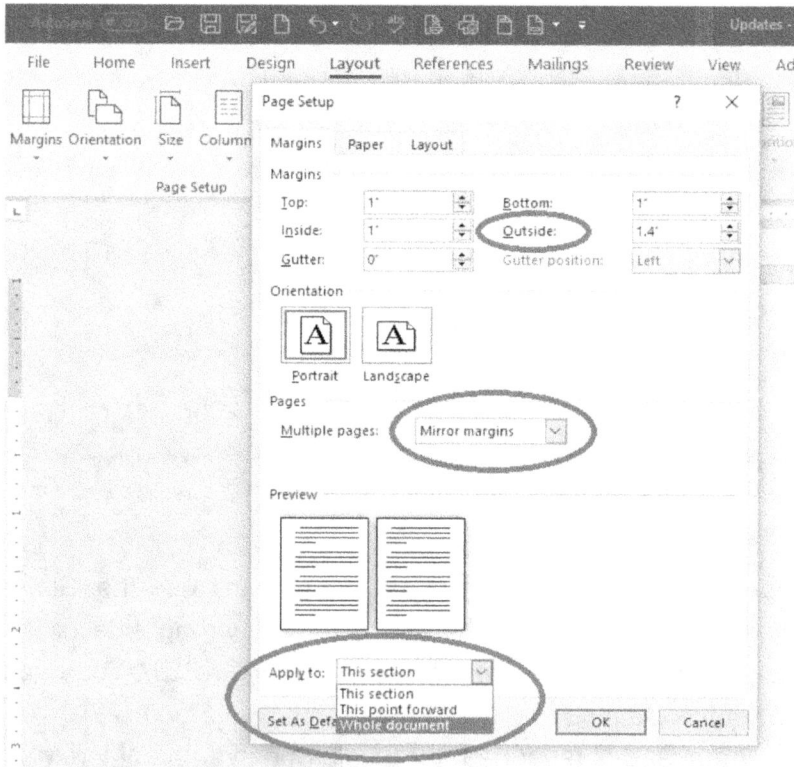

Figure 28 - Using mirror margins in MS Word

Embedding fonts

You will also have to embed fonts. To take care of that, select *File* tab on the main menu and scroll down to *Options*. Click it and then select *Save* on the pop-up menu. Check *Embed fonts in the file* (see *Figure 29*).

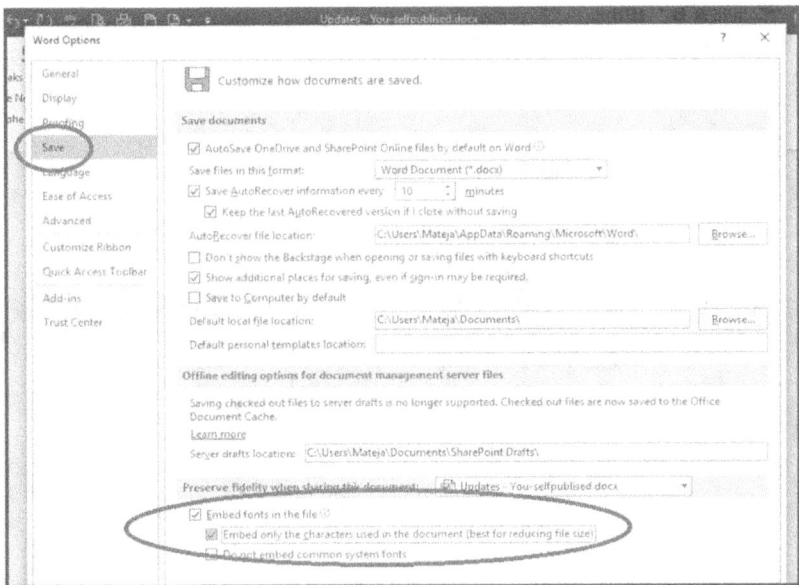

Figure 29 – Embedding fonts in MS Word

Export MS Word file as print-ready PDF

If your book has no images, you can convert your MS Word file into a print-ready PDF by selecting *File* on the main menu, choosing the *Export* option and clicking *Create PDF/XPS Document*. (see *Figure 30*). In the pop-up window, select *Optimize for Standard (publishing online and printing)*, and then click *Options*. Select PDF/A compliant PDF option (see *Figure 31*).

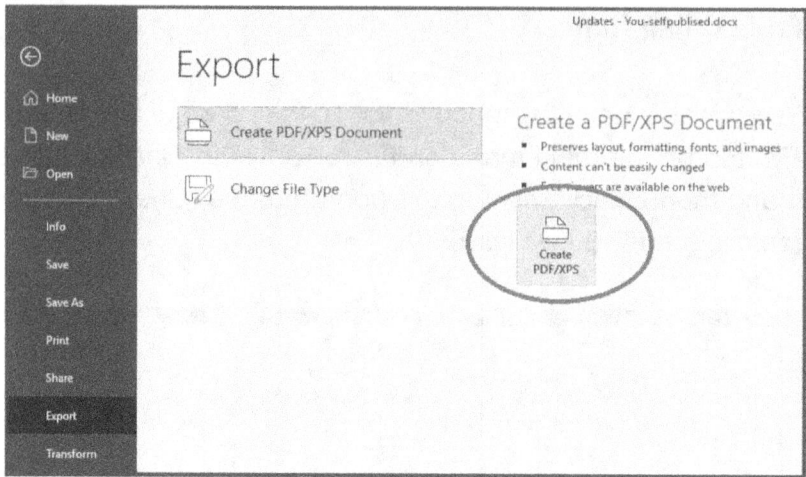

Figure 30 - Creating PDF in MS Word

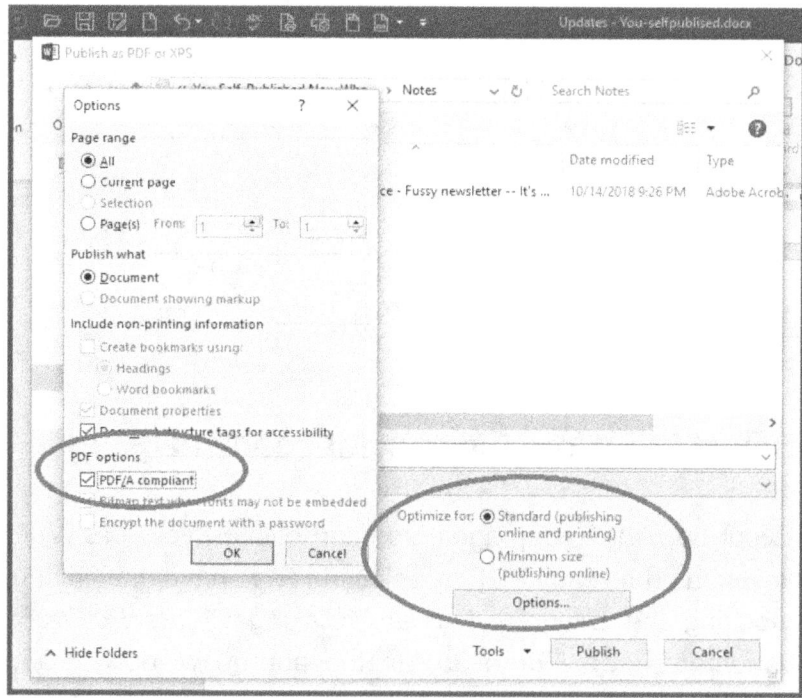

Figure 31 - Creating PDF/A file in MS Word

This option, however, won't be good enough if you have images in your file since MS Word reduces the image resolution during the inbuilt PDF conversion regardless of the settings. In that case, make sure you prevented Word from compressing the images first (see Chapter 7, *Figure 11*) and then use doPDF [21] instead.

doPDF is a free program that converts Word documents into high-quality PDF files. Once you install it, you will be able to use it as one of the printers. To turn your Word document into print-ready PDF with doPDF, go to *File* on the main menu and click *Print.* Find and select doPDF among the printers (see *Figure 32*).

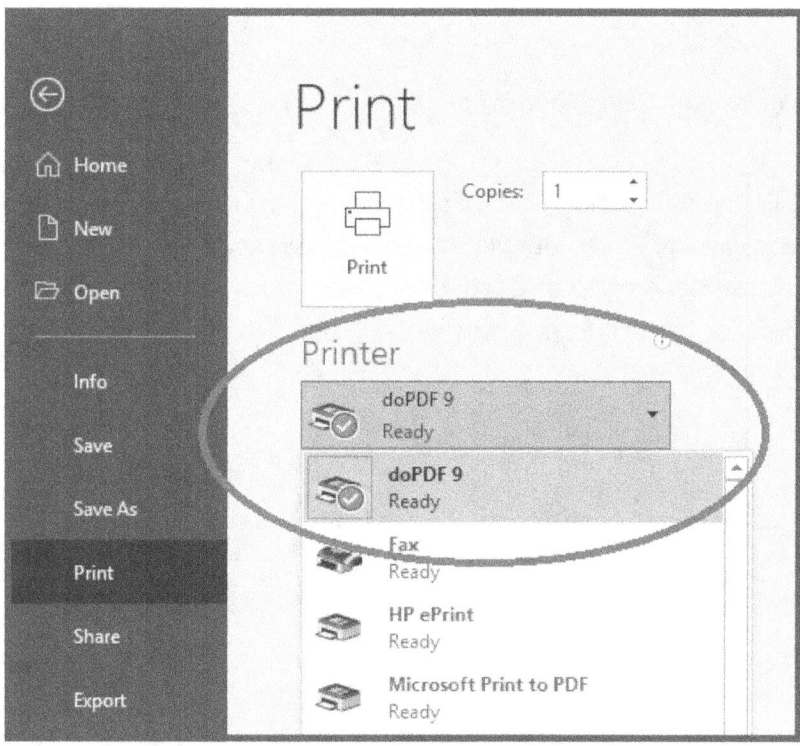

Figure 32 - Using doPDF to create PDF file

Click *Printer Properties* below the *Printer* option. This will open a dialog window where you need to make sure the resolution is set to 300 dpi. Also, set *Custom* size for your book based on the size of your paperback (see *Figure 33*).

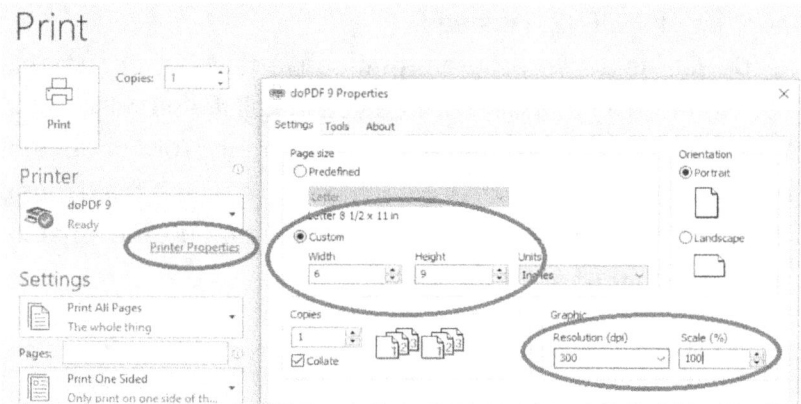

Figure 33 – Setting doPDF properties

Click *OK* and then *Print*. In the pop-up window select where you want to save your file, make sure the quality is set to best, and select embed all used fonts (see *Figure 34*). Click *OK* and wait for the program to convert the file.

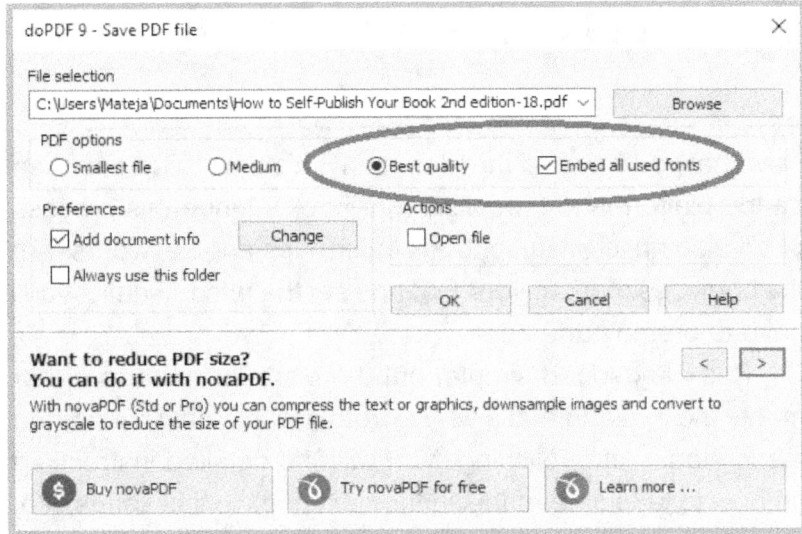

Figure 34 – Setting doPDF print options

10. PUBLISHING YOUR BOOK

Now that you have all the files ready, it's time to upload them on the platforms and publish your book. During this process, you'll also have to select book categories and keywords, add the book description, your bio, and set the price. Finally, you'll have to promote the book.

This may sound simple, but there's a lot more to it than meets the eye and that's why I wrote a whole new book about these stages of publishing. You will find detailed instructions on how to take care of this in the next book in this series, *You Self-Published, Now What? How to Promote Your Book* [2].

But first, create your Amazon Author Central profile, fill it out and make sure to claim all editions of your books (ebook and paperback) – this is important because it will affect how your books appear on the Amazon's product page. You'll find more on this in the second book in this series [2].

Also, it might be a good idea to subscribe to my monthly newsletter on my website (www.matejaklaric.com) since that's where I share new information as well as links to blog posts. Things change fast in the world of online services and that's why I keep my subscribers updated regarding these changes well before I publish new editions of my books.

If you found this book helpful, please spread the word and write a review so that others can benefit from it too. Thank you and best of luck with your self-publishing projects.

References

1

"Books by Mateja Klaric". Books2Read, 2018.
https://www.books2read.com/ap/nOLLz8/Mateja-Klaric

2

"You Self-Published, Now What? How to Promote Your
Book". Klaric, Mateja. Books2Read, 2018.
https://www.books2read.com/promote-your-book

3.

"Best and Worst Self-Publishing Services Rated by The
Alliance of Independent Authors". Alliance of Independent
Authors: Self-Publishing Advice Center, 2018.
https://selfpublishingadvice.org/allis-self-publishing-service-
directory/self-publishing-service-reviews/

4

"How to Find A Literary Agent for Your Book". Friedman ,
Jane, 2017. https://www.janefriedman.com/find-literary-
agent/

5

"Are You Ready to Contact an Agent? Take This Short Quiz
and Find Out". Verrillo, Erica - Publishing... and Other Forms
of Insanity, 2013.

https://publishedtodeath.blogspot.com/2013/05/are-you-ready-to-contact-agent-take.html

6

"Meet Mark Dawson, The Literary Sensation You've Never Heard of". Kelly, Guy - The Telegraph, 2016. https://www.telegraph.co.uk/men/thinking-man/meet-mark-dawson-the-literary-sensation-youve-never-heard-of/

7

"What Makes A $100K Author: 8 Findings Every Author Should Know". Written Word Media, 2017. https://www.writtenwordmedia.com/2017/06/07/100k-author/

8

"What Are Successful Authors Doing? (And How Can You Be More Like Them?) - Written Word Media". Written Word Media, 2016. https://www.writtenwordmedia.com/2016/02/23/successful-authors-can-like/

9

"Survey Indicates Indie Publishing is Pot of Gold for Some, Work in Progress for Many." Force, Marie, and Serra, Cheryl - Marie Force Blog. 2016. http://blog.marieforce.com/survey-indicates-indie-publishing-is-pot-of-gold-for-some-work-in-progress-for-many/

10

"CreateSpace Expanded Distribution: Pros/Cons Discussion". Goodreads Support for Indie Authors, 2018. https://www.goodreads.com/topic/show/12068406-createspace-expanded-distribution-pros-cons

11

"Also Boughts & Also Vieweds May Be Going Away, No Kidding". Kboards, 2018. https://www.kboards.com/index.php?topic=302363.0

12

"Amazon Self-Published Authors: Our Books Were Banned for No Reason". Mangalindan, JP - Yahoo! Finance, 2018. https://finance.yahoo.com/news/amazon-self-published-authors-books-banned-no-reason-134606120.html

13

"U.S. Government Publishing Office Style Manual". Govinfo, 2016. https://www.govinfo.gov/app/details/GPO-STYLEMANUAL-2016/context

14

"The Punctuation Guide". Penn, Jordan. The Punctuation Guide, 2018. http://www.thepunctuationguide.com/about-this-guide.html

15

"GNU Image Manipulation Program". GIMP, 2018.
https://www.gimp.org/

16

"Amazon KDP Cover Templates". Amazon KDP, 2018.
https://kdp.amazon.com/en_US/cover-templates

17

"Digital Pricing Page - Amazon KDP". Amazon KDP, 2018.
https://kdp.amazon.com/en_US/help/topic/G200634500

18

"E-Book Cover Size". Williams Writing, Editing & Design,
2014. https://www.williamswriting.com/2014/ebook-cover-
size/

19

"Design Quality Check". Canva Help Center, 2018.
https://support.canva.com/canva-print/preparing-your-
design-for-print/design-quality-check/

20

"Google Fonts". Google Fonts, 2018.
https://fonts.google.com/

21

"Free PDF Printer". doPDF, 2018. http://www.dopdf.com/

About the author

Mateja started to write short stories at the age of ten and later became a freelance journalist, radio personality, and explorer of the inner worlds. To make life even more fun, she also ran an advertising agency for eight years. Apart from that, Mateja's life resembles a roller coaster ride full of ups and downs and some pretty wild turns. Among other things, her car was destroyed by tanks, and she survived several brushes with death. Mateja graduated in psychology from Arizona State University and is now a writer, photographer, and transformational guide.

matejaklaric.com

Also by Mateja Klaric

Self-Publishing Made Easy, Book 2

You Self-Published, Now What?

How to Promote Your Book

This easy-to-use manual will introduce you to a wide range of affordable options in book marketing and promotion. You will get a list of tips, clear instructions on the DIY ad design for your books, and recommended tools and links to the best book promotion sites. There are no affiliate links since the book is based solely on honest evaluation and sincere satisfaction with these tools and services.

Self-Publishing Made Easy, Book 3

How to Create Your Website:

For Writers and Other Clueless Souls

Dealing with things such as website hosting and finding the best platform for setting up your website can be a daunting and overwhelming task. This book will show you how to navigate the world of websites, domains, emails, hosting services, and SEO* fast, easy, and at the lowest cost. It will also help you avoid many potential pitfalls so that you'll be able to build and run your website easily, safely, and cost-efficiently.

The Fox & White Rabbit, Book 1

The Story of the Fox and White Rabbit

(not your ordinary fable)

The fox leads a cruel and merciless life until one night in the woods changes everything. A chance meeting with magical White Rabbit leaves the fox shaken to the core.

Nothing will ever be the same again.